A RAFT,
A BOAT,
A BRIDGE

A RAFT, A BOAT, A BRIDGE

poems by

Katherine Soniat

Dream Horse Press
California

Dream Horse Press
www.dreamhorsepress.com
Editor: J.P. Dancing Bear

Dream Horse Press
Post Office Box 2080
Aptos, California 95001-2080
U.S.A.

Soniat, Katherine
      A Raft, A Boat, A Bridge
          p.92

              ISBN 978-1-935716-18-1
              1. Poetry

10 9 8 7 6 5 4 3 2 1

First Edition

Cover: "Island" by Suzanne Nessim
http://www.suzannenessim.com/

for LUCAS, *Namo Kuan Shi Yin Pusa*

Come, Kuan Yin, One Who Hears The Cries Of The World.

Table of Contents

iii

Note:

"Garden Alchemy," p. 72:

In 1906, artists Gabriele Munter and Wassily Kandinsky built a home south of Munich in the Bavarian village of Murnau and there began the Expressionist Movement, initially known as the Blue Rider School. As a renowned painter, Kandinsky's reputation tended to obscure the significance of Munter's work and her contributions to that central movement in 20th century art.

Dedication of poems:

"Myrhh" (p15), for Chris
"Raptors" (p31), for Marna
"Bright Blessed Days," (p36), for Gary
"Slowness" (p46), for Olivia
"Abandon" (p54), for Lucas
"Cloud Gardens" (p61), for Robert
"A Wonder" (p65), for Lauren

I thought that by changing towers, I would also change
the ghosts, and that there, a flower would make them
run away.

—Jean Cocteau

May I be a guide for all who journey on the road.
And for those who wish to cross the water

May I be a raft, a boat, a bridge. May I be an isle
For all who yearn for landfall, a lamp for those

Who long for light, and for those who need
A resting place, a bed.

–Shantideva, 8th century India

ONE

REFRACTION

Little was said as we lay there our bodies close.
That was how we started in a room that held space
for daybreak and the few late stars.

But I rose, and it was not from dream. Wrapping
myself in woolens, I wished you a long, slow sleep.

I wished the clocks would stop, the birds fall silent in the trees. Moving
from room to room, I turned each photograph flat, placed a close, warm
breath on every mirror until I made myself and all the background
disappear.

THE MONKEY BIRD

I say, *crow* and watch it fly through the pines,
until, like a hurled inkwell, it sprawls
on my window.

Catch the scent of conversion—not the stench
of burnt feathers and flesh but the notion that this crow
is going places, arrested for now in the body convened.

Gold eyes of a mutant
stare. I stare.
Winger of wind, lingering prophet in trees—

all of us set lose to make impressions on air.

But this crow is pressed on glass. It's lifted out of the moment,
a dreamer's stop for the moment, and already a woman waits at the window,
marking the green avenues as routes of exile or arrival.

Sister with red shoes poised on your feet, can't you see what's before you?

My mouth helplessly fills with *crow*. Across the leagues of sleep, I give
a limitless, underwater shout for raucousness-in-the-pines, any warning
for this cross-the-heart-of-blackness-then-see-what-happens bird

until the morphic-shift begins. A bird's face furs to our more wizened
simian kin:
            dream, the short-winded approach to a heart that beats in us
and once swung through the trees—the other side of the world pinned
for thought and wonder.

MYRRH

The cat jumps on the bed
to lap vanilla cream, the room
thick with incense.

He loves this whiteness at sunset.
It nourishes the bones and tapping heart,

striations in his ruddy fur.

The apartment clouds.
Weariness settles down

like the close of day in the scented centuries
where the bells, full-weighted, peeled,

and old and young on their knees

moved the tongue in earnest.

COSMOS

The valley's pale with cicadas under the moon as sleepless
I toss my leg over a pillow.

                              The deserted villa up the road
pointed to this. All afternoon, I trespassed, one step after another
up the drive of dying cypress, the gardens wild with hollyhock
and cosmos.

A concrete saint rose through the trees, arms skyward, expectant,
head crumbling. And in the dirt was a child's garden of marked graves—
a cat, two dogs, and the plot for turtles. Someone's wish-fraught endings.

When I was young, cicadas pulsed at vespers outside the church like a cult
of loony believers. *Here's the church, there's the steeple; open the door,*
and see all the run-away people.

                              In such dimness I heard organ pipes
as the throat I would have speak to me as a mother. I tried to conjure her
out of that sing-song dark, tried to make her come home.

The tiffany window filled with sun on that mansion staircase: rosy girls
dropped flowers, a cow licked its calf. And behind the house, off in the pines,
the keyhole to the stone tower continued to rot.

                                        That's where I put my nose today.
Bottom of a well. The earth's bottom I breathed, creature restless for the season
to be done, grasshopper fidgeting on a saint's broken neck.

I needed mystery more than a mother. What I could not have comes to lie down
beside me—blue pillow I rock with under the moon.

16

Deep muscular affliction, sundown. Slow dissolve of the road I rushed down to get past understanding there was only so much to make of space, and her brief landing.

A HAPPY COUPLE

Evenings I hung my purple dress on the balcony
while the Portuguese Naval officers in summer whites
walked from the hotel lobby.

They must know the ocean like their front yard,
descended, as they are, from a long line
of the overly curious.

Was that word *wonder or wanderlust*, I thought,
the dress blowing in the wind.

Its gestures were like those of a woman far below, treading
the lit pool water.

Tinted, silk and fluent.

Two fish suggest a happy couple, the Chinese painting manual says.
Fish pupils must be exactly centered to recall the balance of the sea.

That too I considered. After all, my dress had lingered for days without
falling, predicting a longevity in the scheme of things; not lesser things,
just those less material weight.

Each of its moves was nourished by emptiness. I believed this dress
more responsive to immediate goodness than any of the cell-phone inebriates
scurrying down the boardwalk. And when I slipped it on at night, how easily
it assumed the breath of another.

APRICOTS AND ORANGES

Across islands and water I flew,
enclosed in a plane, my body thrust forward faster
than any of the old navigators could have imagined.
One by one, overhead screens in the cabin descended.
A red line crawled the map, our progress mercurial above
the ocean, the drifted landmasses slowly connecting.

That path mocked me, as though I were the one cut down
by a terminal fever, and not the three I'd lost that year—
the dead with their wide swath of disorder. The emptied
closets, each intimacy I lived through, until pushed by silence,

I took to the air, and flew to a stone village where a street dog
licked and knew how to make it better. Her life full of companions,
she walked between fruit stalls and the all-night corner tavern.

DISPERSAL

I watched the lambs closely, their bleats and nudges
beside the practiced ewes. Overnight they were trucked away,
leaving the field quiet beside the farmhouse owned by a woman
I never met. For years her collie had run down to meet me,
the kitchen lit at dawn.

Now I count spikes that still hold the bird-feeders, invitation
hammered into the pines, and by the potting shed torn feed-sacks
spill for animals to scavenge.

On a gray afternoon, I roam the grounds.
Far from here, the sun must be sinking down in gold
as something I hardly knew comes upon the grass
and each dark window.

THE MONGERS

stockpile light years of weapons that speak
of us as a species. Kilotons enough to make
volcanoes wither and redden. Some wear
the black hoods, some assemble as armies.
They come in sizes from young to flatulent
and flabby, each brain threaded with what it
takes to have war mushroom across the planet.
Pumps push oil from the earth. Partakers guzzle
or gloat as the globe heats: sorry soup of wetland,
glacier, and coral. Not to forget, the drowned polar
bear, or coastlines erased by random tsunamis.
And all the self-righteous threats, all the world's
tarnished barter can't make it better. Not even signs
held by men in the subway, *we eat dog food not sushi*,
do the any good. No gurus with auras, or redressed CEOs,
or the joint-chiefs and presidents can alter this one. So it goes,
the poor and meek revisited as bludgeoned Tibetans circling
the sun while the missiles keep falling.

CAMOUFLAGE

It's Ravel now who's crazy according to the news—only a damaged brain capable of *Bolero*'s rolling cadences in a place where caution is never lacking. The blue light's steady on the 911 phone at the edge of campus. Quaint hue near the napping cattle, the big sycamore reaching up as far as summer let it. Sheep wade through clouds in the stream. Some bucolic trick, I think, animals at peace this close to slaughter.

Now there's movement in the trees as the barkbrown-and-squirrelgrays march on me, like the massed woods of Birnam. On command, these Cadets fall down to play war on their bellies. Four hold me in their rifle sights. Another, bored, stacks twigs in the grass. He smiles then tips his camouflage cap, courtly gesture inches from the ground. I stand as close as I ever will to a firing squad—Goya perhaps the next accused, his mind hung out to dry after trying to equate the carnage. Hacked trees. The war-torn stumps of soldiers.

THE CARD TABLE

My father stationed his life between the ocean and sky,
soldier on ship-deck, the world at war. Later he charted
a path to the moon and back, Cape Canaveral rockets
sparkling above the dunes.

Mother had other ideas about the moon—its glow
on the gulf, her cure for any ill. All that foaming
white light, how could she not be deceived?
Her sadness almost glittered.

The two of them arrived at the same place in the end:
Don't let this happen to you, she warned from her deathbed,
under no moon. *I didn't want you to see me like this*, my father
would say, no guides left, high or low.

This afternoon he picks up pieces of a jig-saw puzzle,
refusing to sit at the card table until each humbling
game is shelved in the hospital lounge. The lock
on the ward-door clicks open, then shut.

Seated at the table, my father for the first time
says he loves me. It makes me figure what the three
of us got dealt by war. War bride and baby. The killer
groom shipped off to battles filled with cries no answer
could soften.

A limit to words established. The letters home diminished.

So many bright explosions, who could be heard
across such water?

Mother and I headed south, my crib placed over raw meat
to lure the ticks away. Bloodsucking weather, heat enough
to leave one speechless.

CIRCLE SINGING

A five-year prison term is given to the man with the video camera,
the guy who zoomed in on his girlfriend in stiletto heels as she
stomped a guinea-pig to pieces. Silent violent wriggles, the rough
trades at it again.

At thirteen, blood-flecked and newly breasted, I stood by the
cockfight ring. The man at the barn door pocketed money, clicking
off and on the naked, wiggly-girl lamp he'd received from the madam
who mostly ran the town. He hooted, then spat on his roosters
that died one by one, staring up at the transfixed men.

Before that guinea-pig story caught my eye in the paper, I'd been out
walking, wondering why a woman would leave her bed at sunrise to
lie in the field grass. Propped on her elbows, reading, she lay there
while a cat walked up and down her back.

By noon I'm part of a circle singing "All Things Bright and Beautiful,"
the animals about to be blessed. St. Francis shines in a window.
Ruby of a man under the azure sky. The priest shakes his holy wand
of water. A Russian wolf-hound eyes the parrot who shrieks an
ill-conceived *come and get it*, chinchilla scurrying up the choirboy's
sleeve—the day, for a song, turned darkly musical.

COOL THEATRE: OYSTER PLOT

We had Human Sex at the Lyric, meaning winter afternoons
spent off-campus in the old movie house—a full course of theoretical
male extensions and stylized female parts, our bottoms anchored to the worn
velvet cushions. For three credit-hours, slide shows flashed, professor droning
about penile projections, gender specific lubricants, and the mind (little on that)
began to wander, as if someone's finger were added to velvet, stirring words
into undulant bodily waves.

        The brain lifted the limits, lowered its brow, and
 slowly teeth began to show, a come-on to anything nearby.

Think of a theatre that dark, with the Devil to your right and the deep blue ocean
on your left. Toss off the arm-rests, make quick work of the chairs until the three
of you levitate to roll through the stuffy air of the Lyric, tongues loose as oysters
alive in the mouth

        as you whisper you want more, you want to rise high as the peaks,
the devil forking you up, the sea cresting you farther, bluer . . . tongues slip,
lick the lip open. All of you, one lover of mother-of-pearl.

STREET KISSES

Buzzards drift in autumn circles,

a darkening navel above the country road.

Feedlot. Back lot.
Gaminess fills the dry September air,

sounds of fucking in the hay loft

while the breathier, heavier animals knock about

in stalls below. Bony punches delivered,

restless as a street fight. The shift slow, then steady
to the cities—tight-fisted men on the sidewalk.
Pinch on the butt, tongue in the ear—

far from where the great birds swooped to the road.
Ripe clots.
        Not so different from the hacked-off city blocks,
graffiti smeared from one alley to another.

The nocturnal urge for someone else's finger to stroke the pulse

as the inner folds unfold.
                    Under the streetlamp, a girl opens
to her lover. The corner church clouds with candles,
smoke in the sanctified dark.

HOPPER'S WOMEN

Time for the masquerade, time for a spirit to play and
stretch itself across the light:
                                   Transparent now, he sees
through walls of their house—the end of her smiles,
book on the lap, train ticket to the sun or farther away.

An artist once, he added pigment to a long line of women
who never got past the window. In their Orphan-Annie eyes
his monochromatic melancholy took hold.
                                   Like ghosts,
they dealt with not being seen, and finally were no more
malcontent than a grove of his late-evening pines.

Toward the end, he thought less of ladies and painted
two harlequins—a man and his mate.
                                   Creamed skins
in a red-lip disguise, they're fresh from the long trespass
of insults hurled one against the other.

Comedian and comedienne, they hold hands and smile
till their heads throb.

CLOCKWORK

Ink spills on the sketch in my drawing manual
entitled *Trees Together But Separate*, a design
two trees behind my house took up in spring,
shaping an H. The way of living things.

Limbs extend, lost in late July to something higher,
bluer. The wind blows and, as if hearing a whistle
past the mulberry grove, my dog runs for the forest,
for the musky spell of that direction.

Cinnabar and scarlet of leaves after frost—
they fall down to be sacked and carried away,
as the dead once were on a son's back. A woman
I knew grew older and lighter each day. Each week
she changed bills to silver dollars for the homeless
by the river.

Covered, they looked like musical instruments that winter
in the park gazebo, until a tall man stood in his army blanket
but would not look at me. The same day, a boy at school stared
when asked why he'd killed his kitten, then said he poppawhellied
its head off with a bike because his brother sat on their puppy
in the driveway and bounced.

KNOWLEDGE

On their way to the funerals, villagers stay near the jeep mounted with machine guns. Probably the same guns as those handed out yesterday when the orders arrived to shoot every woman and thumb-sucking child hidden in bushes by the chapel.

Homes to torch, pigs and chickens to kill, terror settling into its aftermath silence. No more stockings to slip over the face, no more guns to disperse by the somebody everyone knows. The man who, with a snap of his fingers, made life vanish.

Today what's left of families file by graves in the rain. Beneath shirts stitched with bright thread, the heart beats on. They know the name of each man who fired at the bushes that shook with the breath of their women and children.

Accused, now it's the mayor who shakes his head and swears—with an umbrella and in a starched shirt—he has only a "generic knowledge" of what the word massacre even means.

RAPTORS

I walk down steps rolled out to the plane, and the smell of garbage
hits me. Piles of it simply dumped on the coast,
I am told.

        Behind the city, the Andes rise where the not-so-simple
humans swarm in shacks above the dazzle.

Blocks and blocks of the wealthy own not the most,
but the healthiest of children,
and the name *Maria* mostly comes first—

                    Maria Isabella, Maria Helena,
so Jesus will spot them as immaculate for awhile. These namesakes of
Blessed-art-thou-amongst-women will never know their hillside sisters
who sleep under crucifixes on a cardboard roof.

Airborne again, I see how distance makes headway through the mountains
look easy.   Roads like whimsical syrup twist through the gorges and over
plateaus where tin roofs blaze with the equatorial sun, each settlement
a surprise slipped into the Andes. Each cleft, a solitude the sun comes
to light—

        jungle first to the east, uproar of tapir and the sherbet-colored
birds. Heat mounts the vines, the stone, then dips into a green glacial lake.
It shines on an avalanche stopped on the baked rock slope.

Ages it took to stack this land on its way through the clouds—sky full
of raptors, earth full of tremors.

THE GARDEN, MOONSET

Dawn, and the Andes rise
with the same sure tints of a child being born,
snow turning from blue
to red.

Wind whips the shrine to the moon and the lesser ones,
thunder and lightning, golden shepherd standing with his gilded
flock of twenty.

Statue with its jeweled sling-shot was no match for the horseborne
greed of Pizarro. No array of spirits save men or their gardens.
They bleed simply, and follow the moon down.

TWO

STICK

Astronomers call for marvels, a cosmic shower
in the pre-dawn sky. But this dog won't be energized
by prediction.
               He won't move to fetch a fresh May stick
or find a healthy mole-rout worthwhile today. A spring
gland pumps in the fields, and the season slides beyond
surface elegy.
               Maybe it's a timely truth that the young
part of this dog has passed. Then his indifference spikes
with adrenaline. He spots the wild ones as they look
slowly up, then snort and bound away.

Deer shimmer through the red-bud.

The dog, a fastball of delight.

Something like a flying stick is at work here, the instant
that makes a body snap into forward.
                             White scuds dip deeper
into the woods, each animal joined to the shadowy prospect
of the next.

BRIGHT BLESSED DAYS

River wind blows a diesel pall
over the bronze general and horse

in the park. Shuffle here, scuffle there,
a conga line curls around the fountain.

They bang coffee tins marked AIDS.
The voice of Satchmo rises past patio

walls: *bright blessed days, dark*
sacred nights over outcroppings

of glass that sharpen each locked
garden's secret. Street vendors mix

ripe red strawberries with shouts
of collard greens, a bucket of

scrub-water slopping down
to the chill spring ground.

The cathedral choir sings
to the prayerful, stained glass

brightening another sad family story.
Palm fronds click dice in the breeze. Hope

against hope. *What a wonderful world*: the crowning
wish scratching its way from Satchmo's earnest throat.

VELOCITY

Quiet eye of the storm approaches. Not long
before the levee collapses, and the river swims

over to meet the lake. Now there's still time to
head north, hours to beat the surge of late summer

flotsam. Take the homeless along for the ride; they're
good guides to the deluge. Tie a rope to the grocery cart

filled with newspapers and the old man's wife he's rattled
around with, hungry for years. Dismiss the custodians of war

who wage politics on the earth with sharp tongues and weapons.
They'll be part of the solution the water comes up with at the end.

Secure the wall safe, the pick-up, its tailgate, mattresses stained with
family misfortune. Honk and yell like everyone else in this slow exodus

of traffic. No two ways of looking at it once the big winds are here. Queen
of spades floats loose from the deck in the spillway, her castle gone under.

No more wee hours to pop awake in, no night-latches left to go clickity-click.
And who knows if they'll ever find the sack of love letters or the notes of suicide

thrown in with the old shoe fit for no one.

THE WAR

I think I said…no, I said *I think it could have been*
better without the war. He said nothing, his head
freshly placed on the hospital pillow. What might
have happened…another *instead or perhaps,*
as if there were a choice.

He didn't move. That's a fact.
He didn't flinch in the metal bed except for wetness
at the corner of his left eye; the one nearest me
as I sat in the mechanized room. The southern
theater of the war, he called it, men at large
on the Pacific.

His room was chilled as an egg laid at night,
while he recollected lives wobbling about:
He was spy for the day on an enemy island.
Then, it was his ship that exploded and kept
sinking, the sky a mad flashing jumble.

Each time he tried to tell the story, the land turned
to water, the air to flame, and his room was a locker
where the body remained, so the mind could fiddle
with zippers on flak jackets.

Hellish, the smells … that said, he fell back in bed.
He and I both were feeling the war—visceral and

torn as a trashed umbilical.

The backlit soldiers, a family of lost parts.

                                        Slowly

sound diminished, fragments of days, the bridges

blown—confusion monitored and recorded.

SOMNAMBULIST

Arias played on the phonograph
where most nights they carried on till dawn.
Room by room, that house pulsed.

Dim parlor for the women who came to apply for jobs
as mother, after the bedside note translated into my mother's
apology for living.

The front stairs appeared remarkably long the morning they carried
her out, half-dead.

Half of something always was leaving. The best part was the blue

parakeet making old world sounds in its cage at sundown—
simple creature settling in when the birds came home to roost.

~

Asleep, it's the animals I try to save, cripples wandering
the late October field.
                        Following harm into the trees and back
to waking life, I press my ear to the heart of my lover.

Then, restless, I walk miles into the country, past a yard where
two stags stand by a rotted card table.
                                    Like the fabled beasts,
antlers bowed, this cast of dream-brethren lap the dew,
the breeze not yet full of me today.

CROW DREAMS

i

She takes off her dress and gloves. Evening rain
settles, and so does she to have a cigarette in her slip
before the bureau mirror. The servant they call Dummie,
the one who can only say *aiyah-baiyah*, holds a tray of drinks.
Both their faces are chained by smoke, and even the lamplight
seems heavier with time. Someday the woman at the mirror
will say she knew this was vanity, as if a photographer
had posed her.

> *Crow flaps from room to room, vase to vase.*
> *Bird in the house, beware. With two bright eyes,*
> *it plays its part, casts doubt on the past and future.*
> *As the crow flies, death is the one short cut,*
> *the sure diagonal.*

ii

She practices arranging that wistful look,
the smoke like tulle, that other woman with the iced drinks
fits dimly into the background. The mirror doesn't register
her expression and can't predict if the pale woman will ever
be a mother. For now, she raises her eyes like a saint.
She can't see the lit pyre of the world around her.
Cannot, cannot, the words her mouth perfects
before the mirror.

The hall clock strikes on the hour. Crow ruffles
its feathers. Men scatter like dice across the woman's
future, her child left alone at night. She will be warned,
as is hindsight's fashion, her mouth opening like a little
bird's, trying to make sense of the air.

iii

She swore she'd finished with the mirror. Even so, she paid for that seating. One man, one woman: a match. Then the child built around a marriage. Contortions. The cracks came as fine lines, and afterwards one eye of the pretty lady never matched the other. And the woman in uniform, who spoke in broken sounds, shattered into seersucker and flesh. Rain at night was meant to stay, to swim all over the future.

Crow gets wind of the road ahead turning red with explosions—
the path a gypsy had pointed out to the smoking woman
years ago, saying that's where a young mother would
fall to pieces. Wings flashed, birds mottled the sky.
She thought she would crack so held her hands
to her ears, waiting.

iv

She suspected the looking glass would get enough of her, the oh-me-oh-my-self-reviews. Finally, lamplight proved nothing compared to the skeletal jags of lightning. And the woman costumed to serve was replaced by others of few words.

Crow flies out the chimney, flushed by the scent of ashes.
In its eyes, images of women pool as they force their way
into something younger and younger—the rubbery,
naked-girl wiggles to make time fit.

THE BEREAVEMENT FAIR

Drinking red wine at sundown, we spoke of tramp spirits,
finally coming to our own wandering dead. Ed told of his father
shouting in his last moments, *Jesus, Mary and Joseph*, wanting
nothing more than the holy family to wave him on to the other side.

Anne made light of her mother in the yellow dress, who sometimes
clarifies in an attic by the sea but only for cousins and never for her.
Then I offered my mother who rarely spoke but kept me informed
of each makeshift departure, one suicide note at a time.

Now I'm seeing how those stories, the sundown-talk, fashioned
the dream I'm trying to scribble; fingers on one hand numb,
something of my broken marriage becoming less visceral perhaps—
my mate telling me to come home, if only to see the wreck
of branches winter left.

Come home—that's what my aunt was saying in the dream—*and do it now*,
another of my mother's exits underway. She wants me on a plane in a hurry
but I say, *can't you understand there are no pre-bereavement fares*.
Telephone held to my mother's lips, she demands I save her
one last time. Who can imagine discounted tickets offered
to a world losing something every moment.

Then another voice joins in, and it's no long-distant aunt this time,
rather, the cleaning woman from school. *A notification*, she nods,
there's a secret in the broom closet. All she does is look at me,
and I know the sorrow felt when they lowered what suddenly
was a mother into the ground. I could not believe it then, nor
now as I stare at that door—the janitorial staff gather around,
pine oil and damp string mops, the mattresses of mourning.

PRESSURE

January eclipse of the moon, blank wafer
that slips into black above the city.

It's our dark of the year. Rain
in a cockeyed southwind mauls

the white atmosphere,
drowning any scheme to set things

straight.
The barometer drops.

Contradictions stand,
mixed message of the foot-up-and-ready-

to-come-down heron.
One-legged elite sure the body will hold

and not tilt in such stillness.
My sleepy mind fills with fissures,

clash of the spheres. Winter chimes
say we're due for a crack—offer

the toe to a tiger and be licked
to your senses.

SLOWNESS

She frowned when she thought of the Andes,
of early mornings full of bells. She laughed at her feet,

the expensive running shoes. Forgetting the fenced yard,
traffic fuming around the corner, the donkey is beneath her

again on the high mountain pass—

     ledge after ledge drops away until she sits still

wrapped in a blanket, the woolly red and blue gods woven
to their starry pinwheels.
                  Slowly mist shifts from the valley.
Bells glinted on goats, and the animal she wears
falls damply heated about her.

HESTIA

arrives with ashes to corner the past.

By the hearth, a family waits—
each attendant breath, the rising
falling mystery.

There, the ancients dwelt on firelight,
their eyes lacquered with ease.

In dream such repose wants to count
when the stars are out and the covers up.
We feel at home like birds in a ruined
cathedral.

Then we wake, pace, grow tired
of waiting, and as always want to head
for the next best-imagined place.

It's in our blood. It's pointed to as across the sea,
beyond the sky. The way out. Each threshold
dark enough to make the eyes grow large.

GOSHEN GAP

Oaks blow above the gully. One leaf, then the next
slides cold orange beneath my shoe.

Winter is a time to be watched and taken in.

Sleet on the wind. Moon on the rise.
For everyone in the valley, this hole in the pitch
hangs overhead.

I've an eye for the moon, for what makes me
weak-kneed. One tilt, and I could be off this side
of the mountain.

The tides know this unearthly pull.

Peaks whiten as far as I can see. At the end of the dirt road
moonlight shines on my fender, on snail tracks in Goshen Gap.

What draws the solitary to light like orphaned things?

Candle on the ledge, leaves spread like marzipan,
and I'm off to another December—
                              Key West fishing boat rocking,
conchs hauled out of the gulf. I heard one on its glimmery-fingered
nightwalk cross our cottage floor. Please be a sleepy shell, I thought,
while it thumped its way toward Christmas morning.
                                        Small rise up,
hard the fall down. Then that crippled pause in the dark made me
want to put an arm to the elbow.

CYCLING

Bridal and umbilical, she walked beside
then behind him.

Glass-kernel woman, bright seed of a child
caught in a heartbeat.

Her fontanel, like the past, was slow to close.
For moments she assembled to check

time tables by day, walk the asphalt at dusk—
routes for each of her makeshift departures.

Glow-in-the-dark ruminations arrived to flicker
at night in the mountains.

She'd pay most anyone to compose her
a better dilemma so called in fate this late

in the year.
It's a spirited season, the end of December

when gold rings and the stitchery loosen.
Voices rise in her sleep, but come to nothing

more than him calling her back.
Such restless cycling should have put the moon

to shame, should have put it out,
so quick was she to latch onto those promises.

She walked up the stone path, turned the knob,
the door shutting behind her. Brief intercession,

her exit again put in motion.

MUTATIONS

Think of that adage where you fade from view, and I forget: *Out of sight,*
out of mind, notions any brainless computer interprets as *invisible/idiots.*
Funny, how that sums us up without referring to the past.

And since I am on the way out, it's interesting to read that quite naturally
you'll spot me in a crowd. Ready or not—the one over there with the bobbed
hair and cat eyes. A sinking spell that words cannot produce.

Perhaps I should loosen up and be a bit more breezy; just exit, leaving thoughts
behind, as if the cranium had a back stoop to loll upon. The answer to your calls
would be easy: your party is *non-compos-mentis*. Not another line to say.

When I do leave I'll go far, maybe back to the early algae to drift around
with cold-blooded kin. There'll be no recollection of dreams, no flash of
last night's venom, nothing lost for me to save.

                              And not a sign of those
times I ran after you, only to turn and be pursued as we changed minds.

LUCID DREAMING

Named the golden girl,
she was brought to the woods
(without blindfold) to visit two beds:
big one for sex, the smaller for dying—
both full of frontier wishes and maps
to nowhere in particular. At first, she
and her guy locked in each other's arms;
life would be spent honoring domesticity
in the pines where they swore by one fairytale
after another. And think how she made herself
suit sublime fancy, while he intently studied
his brain. And so it was this woman grew tired
in a house full of roses that reminded her of the
Still-Wanted List in the fridge: 1) new mattress,
and/or more softness 2) bigger windows for the
constantly changing 3) *The Myth of an Animal
Companion*, revised edition 4) relaxation for
the Photograph Family who grin and hiss *cheese*
on command. But worse were those rapid-fire noises:
"where's the cook, her smile, my shoes, and whose
idea was this big bed anyway?" Just how could her
name be the answer to most every question? On a down
pillow all night she dreams of park pigeons in a war
zone. Their pink eyes flash as the last lover on a park
bench flips her the finger, adding part of his body
to underground longing.

HALLOWEEN

was around the corner when she said she was leaving
and, as the crow flies, so did she straight out the back door
past the straw man stuffed into a sky-blue work shirt
in the stripped autumn field.

Cream soured in the bowl of blueberries. The phone rang
through frigid days, and on into the dark, his pistol holster
hardening in the closet. Sleet hit windows as life as it had been
disappeared.

Later she returned to stand on the hill and think what followed
the wind as it drank in her presence. She pulled a wool cap over
her ears, sure even then she could hear the house, its furnace click
off then on, vines covering the second-storey bedroom window.

ABANDON

The old carousel's reindeer, horses, hares, and one
      snarling tiger are locked to a standstill.
Janus hangs his masks around the mirrored rim—

mocks himself with the smile and eyes of too much
      tropical gin, only to face his day-after, sadder twin.
These animals are burdened by expression. Garlands

weight their necks. I want to blow each like a dandelion,
      blow with the away, away of the season until
the whole herd floats loose, their Sistine tints calling

each about-to-breathe-look into question. Tiger
      is first to shift to a crouch in the pavilion.
Then off with the reins, in with her sinewy stride to the

forest and the steaming dung of others. Scent regained.
      Shadowy cat on the slope licks the wet entrails.
Her glances are quick, the chewing steady—apricot

stripes and black bars of a stealth.

IN THE TAKLAMAKAN

the desert spreads like hammered gold
and translates to

what-goes-in–never-comes-out.

And nothing did, after the festival lanterns
went dark south of Karamay and Shache,

sacrifices made to the god of nether.

Sand trap, air-tight bottle of a tomb that holds
without solace saddest of all the broken babies,
ended headfirst in a dune.

Caught, distraught, this child, this declared artifact
(#0413 of site B)

wears a petrified grimace on her tired mummy lips.

                    She had seconds to snuffle,
then all the time in the world to settle into the jut
of the break in her neck. Little one, lidded, but not

playing possum on the western edge of China.

SWAN SONG

Sleet.   Sled with a broken runner.

Who's out to leash the wolves tonight?

Clouds break   moonlight scopes the earth.

Pale flesh
and the ivory incisors.
        Wolf trots off with a hand in its mouth.

The air's molecular. Vials of mandrake foam on the apothecary shelf.
Torches bloom on the outskirts of a village.

Screams split the atmosphere like atoms.
Where is our lost elixir—ancient essence of *olive and dove?*

Wrist torn off—this wolf runs
from no one.

The sky's striated red and booming   (hearts used to be like that).
Winter moon, another celestial rock above the slaughter.

Stray hand, such a playful toy to toss, lifeline exposed to the elements.
        Morsel map of the old world.

THREE

SOLAR CROSSING

At sunset the beach is a picked pink, almost raw,
seam between worlds—

sea-oats breezily reminiscent of the planet's slow motion.

An island tale, this woman who roams the shore each
September. The villagers know her singing, a voice

that rises then disappears.

At times she has no more to add than the wind to a cage
full of hairy spiders.
                           But once she gets past the factoring—
the ounces and dollars and questionable costs of living—
she swims for the lighthouse.
                                   Hand over hand, then up
the long stair to the room with a wrap-around window.

Sheer solitude, the exactness of one heartbeat. Over
and over, the ocean's resounds on a day set aside

for the sun to fall south in.

INTERLOPERS

All I did was look at the park's stone wall
lined with crumbs for the birds, or perhaps for part
of me—lure that lead my eyes down through the ravine
to a stream stagnant with the hillside wealthy's sewage.

That's where the bushes swayed
and collapsed,
the nose-down, in-and-out dogs running about,
something sacklike fallen from a tree,
me yelling, *ola, scram*, any sound that meant
break it up in a hurry.

The grove was a nest of feral cats the dogs stalked daily.
Thuds and numb screeches, that black fright-wig
I almost tripped over—a dog-gutted cat mashed
to the fence in a park near the ocean.

By afternoon I returned with a friend to hear Liszt
in the amphitheater. No cats hid under the grand piano
or hors d'oeuvre tables shaded by the loquats. Guests
complained of a shortage of vintage champagne,
mist dampening their various lacquers.

The pianist wiped his fingers, then each ivory dry
and twirled to a songbird finish as we headed for the back gate
where we'd walked in for free. High-pronged and locked now,
it barred us but for three bent spears. My friend raised her long
skirt, then her leg, and there two men stood, smiling in the trees.

INFUSION

Pear blossoms cover the lawn—
snowy coat that makes time skip

to keep up. So quickly this April day

goes cold. I think in all directions:

of winter: of fields: of the countryside
abandoned as cities filled with hope, then less,
and less than less—
                              this suburban lawn
my green winter tea. Steeped.

CLOUD GARDENS

I came to the ridge they promised was hard to find,
and there spread the windblown sky and you adrift
in your animal nickname: undulant gray fox of a cloud,
The day probably had to start with you lowered in
at the summit, a late spring front passing through.
All that felt energy of absence.

May gravity hold me in place, I thought, sitting on a ledge,
flies newly hatched and buzzing. The sky set me up after
you'd been gone a year, seeping, receding deeper
into the ground.

Fog lifted from below, the valley spread with cottages
and clotted May gardens—one flagpole taller than the cabin
was long. Red, white and blue unfurled on this moist
Mother's Day.

I wanted to speed by, not touch such family-laden,
chimney-smoked air, so headed my car for the next green
mountain. Under a canopy of leaves, I slowed to hear the creek's
rock-chink splash and hush that lives inside a cloud.

Weightiness settled me, like the heft of taking you in
at the summit until a pick-up hit my bumper. I pulled over.
It pulled up, tinted window rolling down. Two androgynous faces
stared and licked their lips, then raced away, and I came to another
downhill village where the sign CRAEGER'S HOME CAKES covered
the porch between Rambo Drive and Little Dick Lane.

Polarities, inanities, while the poor brainless animals are smashed
into the asphalt. Like mileposts they lead to the church where the man
who cut in front of me screeched to a Cadillac halt. His son sufficiently
yelled at and shoved from the car with his Bible, the guy took off in a self-

righteous cloud. Not your cloud, but it made me think of you and wonder
about the shapes of cunning—"the newly-improved and privately-run"
state prison rising into view—space for men to live and die in.
These mountains wild enough for some to disappear into
for years, unseen

RADIANCE

Bernadette walked from the kitchen singing "Hold On," that song
with a rising refrain. Her voice strong, she looked at us in turn: the
woman with a bullet lodged in her head, one with the daughter dead
a year, another whose unexplained anger flew loose daily. And me,
the visitor trying to come home again.

Song filled the room by the pond, scarlet scarf on Bernadette's head
damp with sweat. Then that ringing, and how I knew to head for
shade by the water. Your voice from a marriage ago. I fingered the
phone cord like something umbilical as it filled with all the clues to
mourning—every word a hot match in my ear. The cancer cells, the
toxins. Doctors had made a mortal chemistry of your body, and you
were ready to leave, radiant as the undeclared dead.

Artesian pool at my fingertips, clouds spring-gray and blowing
overhead. And only moments before we had been speaking of our
bodies. One friend wanted to keep each organ far past the end;
another laughed at her corpse on a pallet at the harvesting center.
And there you were, alive with death eating at you on the other
end of the line.

OCTAVE

The orange cat and twenty plants
depended on me for water, and at dawn the cat
leaned against my ankle, plants to the window.
The pencil cactus tingled when read to from Sarton's
Plant Dreaming Deep, down to its calligraphic roots.

At night the cat shrank to a smirk in the pinion pine,
and should that not be enough, a fern flew spores around
demanding more of itself. That house had twelve windows
and narrow stairs leading up to another level, flap in the door
for one hungry feline. Fur made breezy adjustments to each
flip of the flap.

The plants shed and grew new as the cat's pumpkin eyes
got rounder, life outside shifting from day to night—
or sometimes it vanished completely in floods,
only to surface again to fixate on the sun.
                                        A little like
Mendelssohn when he paced for months in gloom, then
headed precipitously into the octaves and stretch of
composing A Midsummer's Night Dream.

A WONDER

a bird this green and tropical could talk itself home
with human voice in its parakeet throat. Words it let fly
at a stranger in the park: *My name is Petie. Petie,*
then the seven digits of his owner's phone, finished off with,
You got that… got it, huh? And shortly, the whole of TV land
rushed out, only to discover a man coaxing his blinking bird
down from a limb.

I got his got it, and thought I'd gotten it years ago with a child's
sign nailed to the streetcar stop: *One blue and green bird lost
somewhere in the sky. Please return.* I took that as the final
word on run-away birds. Now the lost reconstitute as the
vaguely familiar. Under the eaves on a wet afternoon,
we hear the rustle of what we want to believe.

THE GIVENS

Long passages of light and dark passed before breathing
fell into place. Snake curled on a rock, tail to mouth,
the good lineation.

Lives began to move in their hides, air swimming with the raucous
initial flap of wings as the upright arrived on strong haunches
with a different kind of heart.

He would want to see himself everywhere, in everything, and indeed
would go out looking. *Companionship*, a generous voice called it.
So the wide world went, flashing mirrors at the risen human twins.

Later, clouds blew across the orchards, the wooden boat doused
in rain. Lamentations of the pairs rose through the thunder,
swallow wings aching for tree-to-tree existence.

Far past those animals, who had to wait and could not comprehend
the terms of deluge, comes this tale of snakes—the circle broken,
reassembled as headlines: VANLOAD OF SNAKES

FOUND SMOTHERED. Rectums sewn up, bellies stuffed
with condoms of cocaine. Swelter of metal. The back-alley heat.
But before that, someone had to look hard to thread a needle, then

stitch each snake's tiny puncture shut, fingers forcing last rubbery
meals down creatures' throats. Glitzy city full of people in sunlight—
this planet we walk on, a place where the tale began quite naturally

with animals and water.

LINCOLN DREAMING

Petals fall from a vase,
four days and they're gone.
What to include in our newly
emptied space? Enter Lincoln,
the cat, battling with a screen door.
He wants in to the meditation hall,
into this void we've so assiduously
have created, one breath at a time.

Summer cat flops on the wooden floor.
And he might never move again in this life,
or any of the ones to follow. The shadow
of his ear darkens the polish, the other
twitches in dream as, lo, the four messengers

appear: old man, sick man, laid-out corpse. then
the wandering wise one with staff and begging bowl.
Breath quickening, Lincoln signals he relishes that dish
and won't wait it out under a Bodhi tree.

CASSANDRA

Trouble goes and comes, unsteady
quivers at sunset, then down falls the night-tableau—

and I am there, alone and wandering between sky-high
elephant legs. I alone comprehend the sway

of possibility.

Oh me, oh my birdlike, one true view.

But dreaming is never that simple and, of course, here
she comes—peasant from the sleep garden, changing the story
around with her basket of greens. She beckons the elephant.
Here, little one, the woman calls, shaking her fronds.

Its great ears flap.

They fan the dust, the air, I'm given to see through.

FORTUNE

i

In the mine, a man's eyes belong to the panther. Wariness
in a circle of black.

Something with teeth marks him as feline
designed to tunnel for life; an energy with talons straps
the lamp on a poor man's head,

then drives him down on an empty belly.

An old surgery, these men who try to cut veins and
breathe air inside a mountain.

ii

Rag-heap-of-flies sits up in the hut, rubs its eyes. It's a boy.
One day his thoughts may catch fire and brighten, until

he wants more than the family pig at the door, garbage-slide
down to the highway.

Rainbow flags blow from the market stalls stacked with sacks
of coca leaves. Not a ceremonious chew but enough to dull

the hungry stomach. Leaves at the bottom of a cup tell of
children who flicker and go out on the slopes

while the miners go under.

WILD APPLES

She walks among the apple trees. Sometimes a hillside man,
or is it a black column of air, comes with binoculars to track her.
Then he reverses them, shifting her to a speck.

> She knew she'd spotted trouble
> that day he talked her back into the house
> and spoke of setting the end in motion—
> the house a pyre.
> She rubbed her hands together, put on red.
> Cold sparked in his eyes.

Love starts to decompose with the eyes.
Something missed,
was missing, and she went on saying
look at me. Perhaps I am being unclear,
not driving the point home
or *where do you want me to go*
and *I want you to go . . .*
Words flew about like that.

> I think her scarlet scarf is mine,
> and there he is, the tall one, reaching for it,
> his hand like a match going for her hair.
> She blows out one last long breath.

I breathe in and see her hurry off through the garden.
He's smoked her out, beaten the bushes—his threats,
like a bite out of anything frail and lit inside. *Burn it*
down to the ground. That's how he put it to her,
their house on the ground.

There was another way it came apart.
She lay there, rearranging the bedroom shadows,
trying to get comfortable. He backed the car out
on the hour, over and over, and the clock chimed in
like a missing mother jiggling the night latch.
Tinkering to get back in.

Watch out, I thought, he's leaving her empty
and full of an old formula she'll put her mouth around.

GARDEN ALCHEMY

i. I painted one good and two poor studies. Our house was one of the former.
   Out of this world.   —Gabriele Munter

Thoughts of cold came by mid-October, the flowerpot for her sandals overgrown
with dahlias. Shoes in a someday pot-of-snow. They had a place on her canvas,

along with him digging in the garden behind their stucco house. She sketched him
in profile—like a mountain rising from the ground, on edge in his straw hat.

She lived through the garden, slept in it with him and the trees. In one self-portrait
her eyes come off as a bit too bright among the blossoms. Not blossoms, the eyes

are in need of correction.

Wind made the guinea hens restless, a crane's ivory cry floated down through
the rain. And there she was running through their orchard. Rotted apricots

bruised her feet as autumn passed from red to dark-pooled scarlet. With it
came the dream of blood turned to snow in the one leaving.

Such thoughts made the clouds look lower. Small ones with dark centers,
like her feet at night in the orchard. A fox barked so she painted it a path

to the chickens as she began to fall away, or fall asleep, drifting toward
the doorway that swam in muted blues, always dissolving.

White is an absence that goes without saying, the lesson bitten down on hard
until it cracks like ice between the teeth. And the mountains seemed so soft

that last winter—ridges of blown powder on moist silk.

She kept the sequined bag they'd sewn for phrases: "... fisherman stares
at the clouds from his watery estate"; "... spring nest on the lip of a chimney."

The fact was the garden changed when she'd brushed the vireo's eye with red,
then the cracked tortoise shell—geometries that fit, and ones that don't quite

make it into the picture.

ii. he (Kandinsky) said he'd never seen such perfect yellow as in my paintings…
he once saw my personality as this warm yellow.   —Gabriele Munter

Perhaps she thought, *I am sad and the world's absorbed*
with color. Sparrows at sunrise tired her, the lake
a pale blue.

Who knows when separation first began—something made her
go to sleep when daylight was its thickest yellow.

See her

on the ground, one arm across her eyes, the quilt's saffron patches
sewn tightly beneath her.

And though her ankles seem part of the painting, they're only suggestions—
an absence of color between the curved tulip leaves.

As with dream, the void angles in.

If you roll her on her side, she's just another black hip of a mountain,
the tulips doing their best to constellate her lost parts.

Darkness and threaded gold patterns, cross-stitch flare
of the universe.

Strange, she's not moved by such passing fancy.

iii.   dear Was

Afternoon ravens fly about cawing for rain in our September garden. There's dust in every corner of the house, the streambed dry, and Alpspitz's peak beyond the gate is barely visible through clouds of gnats.

Your favorite pickert I left uneaten—the chopped potatoes, pancake batter and raisins in bowls on the stove. Instead I went out early to watch the red roof by the lake intensify at sunrise. The corn is cut, hay rolled and stacked in the field, the way you like it best—far away from the train tracks. I suppose they will always be our home's curse. The daily blur of faces that speed by. But fewer come now for the weekend from Munich.

On days like this the forest is a parched green. I hold dry earth to my nose, and breathe. It's only a short distance, you remember, through those pines to the forester's abandoned cabin. If you were with me we could marvel at the shades of dark in that empty room—the high hewn rafters of cedar. I'd slip off my thin blouse and white skirt of voile.

The food-line in the village is long and everyone's dirty. Thirst now to add to hunger, and here I am remembering our love on a dead man's wooden floor. A dreamer, I learn to watch my thoughts, perhaps to wait and listen.

The roses by the porch are finished, apricots a shriveled yellow, and this afternoon, indeed, is my time "to bare the knees," as you used to say. I sit on the tool-shed steps, skirt up, a pail of what's left of the gooseberries at my feet. And so, I wonder about you and about these words I write— blue ink on white. Something of the sky, and perhaps us too, is turned inside out.

your Ella

iv.   I have a yearning—for what I do not know—often I feel like a figure
in one of your paintings.   —Wassily Kandinsky

That night she cut her hair and turned from the window.
A tube of antique gold by her palette marked the time of day
the man from Mineral Street arrived in dream to float about
with his bottle and flowers.
                      Chagall's flame-haired angel
looking for company, looking for his own demise
on which to place those roses. Constant, his need
for celebration and for endings.

Sometimes she rode the train home from Munich.
In her lap, the purse they'd stitched together one winter—
pearls on a velvet lake,
her long hair recalled by pewter combs at the bottom.

You'd get a better sense of her by saying *apricot, almond,*
and *olive* over and over, if the heart's in it. Hers was skimmed

off by brandy beneath the arbor— *drink*, he said, and they did,

and bottled wings grew like a family feature.

v. . . . my mountain landscape with pines, the train tracks and
      straight road, then there's our house near Murnau again.

Years afterwards, she returned to paint sheep in the pasture
on her side of town—the right, to be exact, should a moor
with houses have sides like the brain.

Rain over the Alps, soggy flocks loose in wolf-clover.
The land absorbs a rueful eye. Twilight, a constant
in the world's gray muscle.

Complete, her self-portrait in the brimmed hat—
pendant like Eve's lump-red heart hung at her throat,
half her face left in shadow.

Their house still sits near two sets of tracks, north
and south bound. Whistling in the dark on every side.
Something remains at odds on her canvas—bright eye,

then the would-be evening-one planted in umber.

vi. . . . and so she

walks across the tracks, unlatches

the garden gate,

autumn spotting the leaves darkly golden.

The veil dissolves between her and the land—the moors
soak her up, muddy sheep in a huddle. Some moves she never
got straight

his comings, her goings, then the reverse.

The parlor lamp was a still point in its red-beaded shade.

Fidget-of-heart faltering this way and that.

Her brushes are ready. A few strokes, and the garden
will sink under a pall thick enough to scratch.

vii. clouds

The road to the depot is lined with poplars,
field stones warmer this afternoon
than anyone's hand on the shoulder.

So much for the turtle in its shell
filled with the body's old proclivities.

Daily, this roam in the sheltering cell,
hourly the conflagrations that hold us there.

A stray sniffs for home in the garbage.

The lake reflects the powdered white

of implausible beings.

THE CELEBRANTS

The police lieutenant said flatly that the gathering was canceled.
He gave no reason why.

—account from a celebration for the deceased poet
Antonio Machado, February,1966. Baeza, Spain.

The poet's cranium under a dust-cloth, its bronze eyes fixed

on Baeza. Men and women ready for a day of homage in the park.

The festival is alive with buses and horns, a celebration that grows

shrill then starts to tilt,

bullhorn roaring

> *canceled*

> *disperse.*

The morning turns to a scramble of faces, La Guardia herding people,

shoving with rifles. Constable's breath on the neck. Hot, sour,

snorting *basta*.

~

1939: Earlier moves on the road. Car driving north,

dust-lengths ahead of Franco. Machado riding shotgun

bundles his old mother on his lap. A long afternoon

for this Madonna and child.

~

In Baeza, Machado's head is cast in bronze. The constable takes

a step back from the crowd.

He blows twice, then lets his silver whistle

drop and joins in with the clubs and guns. A woman nearby scribbles

80

"how glorious that man's pistol is to him. He waves it as if he were fencing. Furious, and absolutely out of his mind."

Canceled.

Disperse.

Out of the question to ask questions, these heads knocked no harder than any in the past, chaos shaken out with the keepsake-ease of one, two, three.

CRIMSON LAKE HOUSE

The home-place returns, and it's his
eyes that shift in the crosshatched pines,

part of a primary haunting.
This, the first space/person recollected—

the unspoken room by room of it. Blue print
of a father's face at every window. She climbs

from cellar to attic where shadows stretch and
the doll-cries are broken.

Round window looks out on the lake.
Blurred quiver of glass, a deformation

of sorts. His better-to-see-you-with parts
dilate, twittering twilight closing in again.

She had to see this house once more
imply like a slice of the family portrait—

incubus in the smudged lower corner
who's-who of the stud-stable breathing . . .

feel the dead weight of a dead star
the first star hung until morning.

SPIT

Necklace of lake air,
and the chains I flew from went high and higher
as my husband called me down.
                                        But I was going after her,
trying to coax her back from the dry-socket ground. I swung
out toward the stars the night of my mother's funeral. Velocity
by the lake. Arcs above the dirt.

                        ~

On the cold Valentine's Day my father died,
I watched the clouds
recede.
I had had his eyes for such a long while by then.
They said I was his spit.
I could hardly believe each swiftly vanishing cloud,
or that long-ago him
                        walking through the front door
after the war.
                A man come home to meet the child
with his eyes—my huff of a father, blown in from the Pacific.

                        ~

What you think of this, another man asked—
                                        flesh flipped
from his fly in the park pavilion. How does one think of
his penis as a child walks up the brown wooden steps,
then come up with the right shady question?

                        ~

Do you really like all that?
He pulled at hair poking from my bathing-suit
leg, scissors ready.
                  Too long, he said as he snipped
                        and I stood like a rock,
or was a rock on some far island beyond this hand.

~

I fell for the holy smoked fragrance of churches—
my cup of whole milk, blue plate of bread.
That cleaned, hands-off smell of altar brass settled me
in a pew.
          I should have stayed there my first twelve years,
breathing easy as a kept secret, or a relic.
But hair grows on the dead.

~

Under the soggy towel,
I felt like something being collapsed to throw away.
The attic fan rattled
                  while I tried to catch my asthmatic breath—
vaporizer bubbling a sickly licorice odor from the bathroom sink,
and I sucked in hard.
                This small face-down death of mine had no profile,
my shrouded head rising and falling as the air seeped in.

~

The hollow oak grew on the convent grounds,
the Virgin's shrine built before it:

                                              Lady with palms upturned,
recipient of rain.

                        Inside her tree we peered up at a patch of sky.
My girlfriend would not tell what she'd found out, but "never,
ever would do, even with her brother."

June-green frog days,

                            egg-threaded dreams,
trying to make the pieces fit that summer.

                  ~

With a sheet wrapped around his body, Brother River
dunked his congregation's heads under, only to have them
spring back holier from the Mississippi.

                                    My stepfather said
one day my mother'd get knocked flat as she walked the levee
with her flashy rings.

                        For weeks, she'd keep to the city blocks
then head for the water again where a man sang to his Jordan
and diamonds caught the sun.

                  ~

Who'd have thought at fifteen I would have stopped to buy her
orange gladiolas for Mother's Day, after coming home at six in the morning?
Friends said I had a dream life,

                                        never told to do a thing.
Most times I think I've lived alone since birth
as each reassembled house fills with those who never know I leave.

                              ~

Afterwards, his presence must have flown out the third-floor
cloakroom window.
                        The janitor's son.
                        Shadow in the dark,
he was part of that man in the park. So quickly both of them
escaped to return in dream—head back, breath held in a cloakroom
of wet wool and boot rubber.
                                    This me, or she—that over-there girl
with her mouth zipped up. He was out to steal pie-sized pieces
of the mind, fractions.   Top half over the bottom and
ready to flee.

                              ~

My regret beckons sad fingers in the wind.
                  I was not there the day she died
and sheets of rain fell across the ocean.

In the most moist part of the year, I find the one
snapshot of her and me left.

Young, hair flying, the two of us standing on a dune.

Cut-outs. End to the tissue-doll life.

~

That Valentine's Day he left for good, I wondered
who was outside the window with an inverse bellows,
clouds inhaled by the cold blue sky.

                             The fire had gone to embers
when they called to say his life was done.

                                  My face flushed with heat,
and I drank glass after glass of water as if I were drifting farther away
from Earth and its clouds, shape sucked out of it all, spit shining
back in the wind.

WORLD DRIFT

A freighter sits on the ocean for days, and at dark it seems
to lose substance, bridge lights sprinkled in with the starry
Atlantic.

For some, staring is enough to complete erasure,

world-drift held at the periphery.

One ship centered on the imperceptible curve of the sea.
I hold my finger up to reckon how truly things stay in place.

Each night we watch the rising constellations, shifts so small
they make us think we are all that changes in the red-roofed
villages that pock the coast.

Those not long for this world gaze out as if the Earth were flat.

Smooth silent horizon.

A lighthouse spins the emptiness out—brilliance that makes
the waves look partial, and all this ocean manageable.

ACKNOWLEDGMENTS

Many thanks to the editors of the following journals in which these poems first appeared:

Anthology of Southern Poetry, Louisiana: "Bright Blessed Days"

Arts and Letters: "Myrrh"

Bellingham Review: "Spit"

Bomb: "Infusion"

Boston Review: "Goshen Gap"

Boulevard: "The Card Table"

Colorado Review: "Wild Apples"

Common Wealth: Anthology of Contemporary Virginia Poetry: "Pressure," "Apricots and Oranges"

Congeries: "Octave"

Controlled Burn: "Halloween"

Crazyhorse: "Interlopers," "Pressure," "Velocity"

Five Points: "Stick"

Green Mountain Review: "Dispersals"

Greensboro Review: "The Bereavement Fair"

Hamden-Sydney Poetry Review: "Abandon,"

Image: Art, Mystery, and Faith: "The Givens," "A Wonder," "Radiance"

Literary Review: "Hopper's Women," "Swan Song"

Luna: "Crow Dreams"

Mid-West Quarterly: "Slowness" (entitled "The Bright Air")

New England Review: "Cosmos" (entitled "Blue Hour")

New Orleans Review: "The Celebrants"

Northeast: "Hestia"

Poet Lore: "Garden: Moonset"

Poetic Voices Without Borders, An Anthology Vol. 2: "Raptors," "Fortune"

Poetry Daily: "Cool Theatre: Oyster Plot"

Prairie Schooner: "Crimson Lake Red," "Solar Crossing"

Quarterly West: "Somnambulant," "Raptors"

Red Mountain Review: "Clouds"

Shenandoah: "Camouflage"

Southern Poetry Review: " Mutations"

Southern Review: "A Happy Couple," "Circle Singing" (entitled "The Circle")

Spoon River Poetry Review: "Apricots and Oranges," "Garden Alchemy"

Superstition Mountain: "Fortune"

Tiferet: "Lincoln Dreaming"

Verse Daily: "Dispersals"

Virginia Quarterly Review: "Monkey Bird," "Cool Theatre: Oyster Plot"

Witness: "World Drift"

Women's Review of Books: "Cycling," "The War," "The Cloud Garden" (entitled "The Fox")

Writers Forum: "Cassandra"

Yellow Silk: "Street Kisses"

Thanks to the Corporation of Yaddo and to the MacDowell Colony for residencies that made the completion of this manuscript possible.

About the Author

The Swing Girl was selected as Best Collection of 2011 by the Poetry Commission of North Carolina (A.O. Young Award). *A Shared Life* won the Iowa Poetry Prize given by the University of Iowa Press, and a Virginia Prize for Poetry selected by Mary Oliver. Her fourth collection *Alluvial* was a finalist for Library of Virginia Center for the Book Award and Notes of Departure won the Camden Poetry Prize, selected by Sonia Sanchez. Soniat has served on the faculty at Hollins University and Virginia Tech. Currently an instructor in the Great Smokies Writers Program at University of North Carolina at Asheville, she lives on a deep ravine with a mother bear and two cubs.

www.ingramcontent.com/pod-product-compliance
Lightning Source LLC
Chambersburg PA
CBHW022030090426
42739CB00006BA/358